OTHER BOOKS IN THIS SERIES:

For a wonderful Mother A book to make your own
For a wonderful Grandmother A book to make your own
For a real Friend A book to make your own
A Girl's Journal A personal notebook and keepsake
A Woman's Journal A personal notebook and keepsake
Cats A book to make your own
Teddy Bears A book to make your own
A Gardener's Journal A book to make your own

OTHER INSPIRING HELEN EXLEY GIFTBOOKS:

Wisdom for the New Millennium
Words on Hope
Thoughts on... Being Happy
Seize the Day!

Published in hardback 1990. Published in softcover 2001.
Copyright © Helen Exley 1990, 2001
Selection © Helen Exley 1990, 2001
The moral right of the author has been asserted.

12 11 10 9 8 7 6 5 4

ISBN 1-86187-217-8

Selection and design by Helen Exley
Illustrated by Juliette Clarke
Printed in China

Exley Publications Ltd, 16 Chalk Hill, Watford, Herts, WD19 4BG, UK.
Exley Publications LLC, 185 Main Street, Spencer, MA 01562, USA.
www.helenexleygiftbooks.com

Acknowledgements: The publishers are grateful for permission to reproduce copyright material. Whilst every reasonable effort has been made to trace copyright holders, we would be pleased to hear from any not here acknowledged. Dawna Markova Ph.D.: From *The Art of the Possible* © 1991 Dawna Markova. Excerpted from *A Grateful Heart* by M.J. Ryan. © 1994 M.J. Ryan, by permission of Conari Press. Gloria Naylor: From *Inter/View: Talks with America's Writing Women* by Mickey Pearlman and Katherine U. Henderson. © 1990 The University Press of Kentucky. Nadine Stair: From *The Unknown Region* ed. Eileen Campbell. Published by Aquarian, an imprint of HarperCollins Publishers.

Inspirations

A BOOK TO
MAKE YOUR OWN

A HELEN EXLEY GIFTBOOK

EXLEY

You have powers you never dreamed of.
You can do things you never thought you could do. There are no
limitations in what you can do except the limitations in your
own mind as to what you cannot do.
Don't think you cannot. Think you can.

Throw your heart out in front of you
And run ahead to catch it.

Make voyages. Attempt them. There's nothing else.

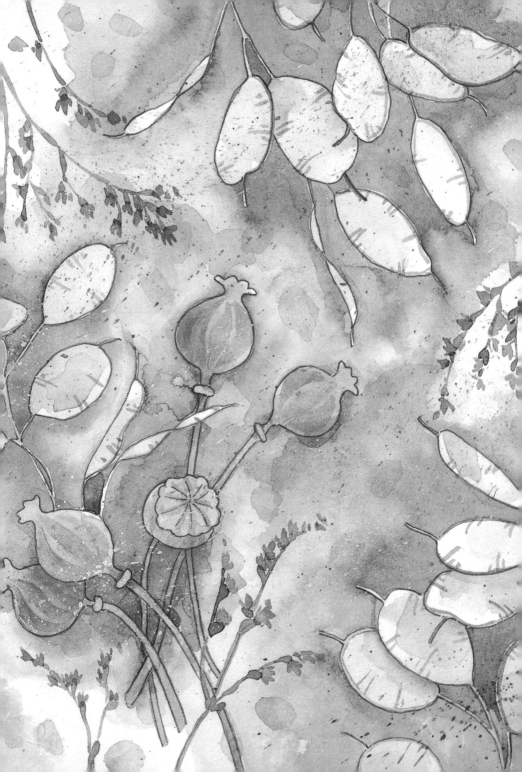

... $\mathcal{I}$ choose to inhabit my days,
to allow my living to open me,
to make me less afraid,
more accessible,
to loosen my heart
until it becomes a wing,
a torch, a promise.

DAWNA MARKOVA

You can have anything you want if you want it desperately enough. You must want it with an exuberance that erupts through the skin and joins the energy that created the world.

SHEILA GRAHAM

Nothing great was ever achieved without enthusiasm. The way of life is wonderful; it is by abandonment.

RALPH WALDO EMERSON (1803-1882)

Your enthusiasm will be infectious, stimulating and attractive to others. They will love you for it. They will go for you and with you.

NORMAN VINCENT PEALE

L IFE LOVES TO BE TAKEN BY THE LAPEL AND BE TOLD:
"I AM WITH YOU KID. LET'S GO."

MAYA ANGELOU, B.1928

If you can walk you can dance.
If you can talk you can sing.

ZIMBABWE PROVERB

The word "impossible" is black.
"I can" is like a flame of gold.

CATHERINE COOKSON

To laugh is to risk appearing a fool.
To weep is to risk appearing sentimental.
To place your ideas and dreams before the crowd is to risk their loss.
To love is to risk not being loved in return.
To hope is to risk disappointment.
But risks must be taken because the greatest risk in life is to risk nothing.
The person who risks nothing, does nothing, sees nothing, has nothing
and is nothing.
They cannot learn, feel, change, grow, love and live.

AUTHOR UNKNOWN

The secret of making something work in your life is, first of all, the deep desire to make it *work*: then the faith and belief that it can *work*: then to hold that clear definite vision in your consciousness and see it working out step by step, without one thought of doubt or disbelief.

EILEEN CADDY

$\mathcal{D}$evelop interest
in life as you see it; in
people, things, literature,
music – the world is so
rich, simply throbbing with
rich treasures, beautiful
souls and interesting
people. Forget yourself.

HENRY MILLER (1891-1980)

Life is a great big canvas;
throw all the paint on it you can.

DANNY KAYE (1913-1987)

I think that wherever your journey takes you, there are new gods waiting there, with divine patience – and laughter.

SUSAN M. WATKINS, B.1945

$\mathscr{F}$ollow what you love!... Don't deign to ask what "they" are looking for out there. Ask what you have inside. Follow not your interests, which change, but what you are and what you love, which will and should not change.

GEORGIE ANNE GEYER

*Far away there in the
sunshine are my highest
aspirations. I may not reach
them, but I can look up and
see their beauty, believe in
them, and try to follow
where they lead.*

LOUISA MAY ALCOTT (1832-1888)

*Mama exhorted her
children at every
opportunity to
"jump at de sun."
We might not land
on the sun, but at least we
would get off the ground.*

ZORA NEALE HURSTON

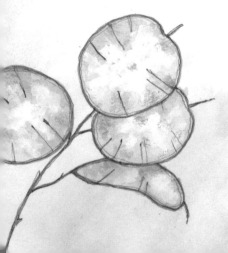

I have a lot of things to prove to myself. One is that I can live my life fearlessly.

OPRAH WINFREY

*H*ow far do you want to go? Go the distance! Within each person is the potential to build the empire of her wishes, and don't allow anyone to say you can't have it all. You can – you *can* have it all if you're willing to work.

ESTÉE LAUDER, B.1908

It had long since come to my attention that people of accomplishment rarely sat back and let things happen to them. They went out and happened to <u>things</u>.

ELINOR SMITH

There are no shortcuts to any place worth going.

BEVERLY SILLS, B.1929

... if you want something very badly, you can achieve it. It may take patience, very hard work, a real struggle, and a long time; but it can be done.

MARGO JONES (1915-1955)

It seems to me
that we can never give up
longing and wishing,
while we are thoroughly
alive. There are certain
things we feel to be
beautiful and good, and
we must hunger after
them.

GEORGE ELIOT
(MARY ANN EVANS)
(1819-1880)

No pessimist ever
discovered the secrets of
the stars, or sailed to an
uncharted land....

HELEN KELLER (1880-1968)

BUT WARM, EAGER, LIVING LIFE — TO BE ROOTED IN LIFE —
TO LEARN, TO DESIRE TO KNOW, TO FEEL, TO THINK, TO ACT.
THAT IS WHAT I WANT. AND NOTHING ELSE.
THAT IS WHAT I MUST TRY FOR.

KATHERINE MANSFIELD (1888-1923)

*When I'm old I'm never going to say,
"I didn't do this" or, "I regret that." I'm going to say,
"I don't regret a thing. I came, I went, and I did it all."*

KIM BASINGER

*And so what I've learned in the last twenty years is that
I am the sole judge and jury about what my limits will
be. And as I look toward the horizon of the next twenty
years, it is <u>no</u>... <u>no limit</u>. With that kind of knowledge,
I've grown as old as I can possibly be; the aging has
stopped here, and now I just grow better.*

GLORIA NAYLOR

I am only one,
But still I am one.
I cannot do everything,
But still I can do something;
And because I cannot do everything
I will not refuse to do the something
that I can do.

EDWARD E. HALE (1822-1909)

It isn't a calamity to die with dreams unfulfilled,
but it is a calamity not to dream.... It is not a disgrace
not to reach the stars, but it is a disgrace to have
no stars to reach.

BENJAMIN MAYS

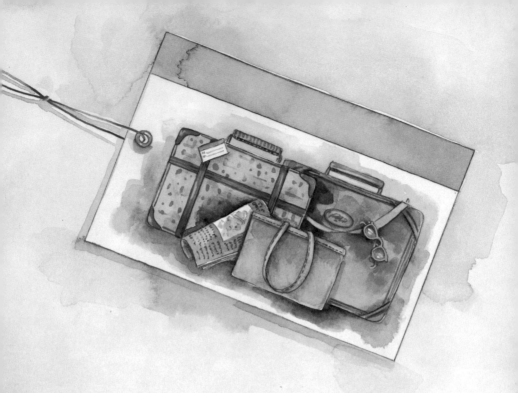

LIFE IS LIKE A WILD TIGER.
YOU CAN EITHER LIE DOWN AND LET IT LAY ITS PAW ON
YOUR HEAD — OR SIT ON ITS BACK AND RIDE IT.

INDIAN PROVERB

D̲o noble things, do not dream them all day long.

CHARLES KINGSLEY (1819-1875)

If we wait till we're ready, we never do anything.

ELEANOR ROOSEVELT (1884-1962)

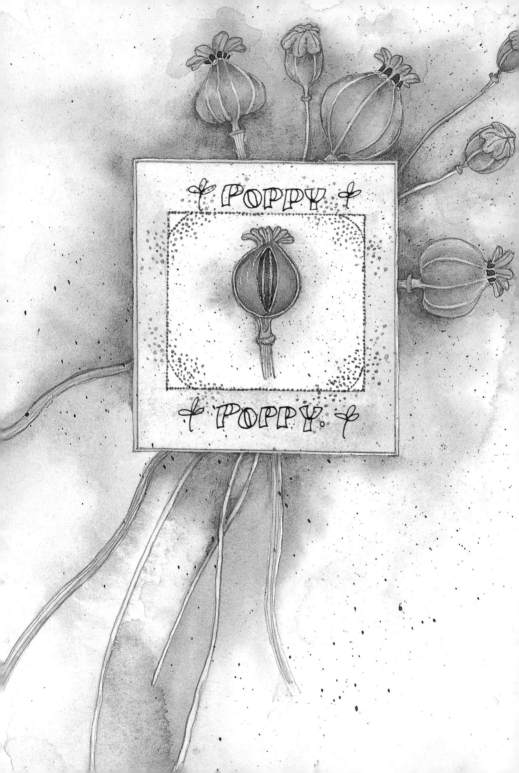

If you come to a fork in the road, take it.

YOGI BERRA

You learn that, whatever you are doing in life, obstacles don't matter very much. Pain or other circumstances can be there, but if you want to do a job bad enough, you'll find a way to get it done.

JACK YOUNGBLOOD

If we didn't live venturously, plucking the wild goat by the beard, and trembling over precipices, we should never be depressed, I've no doubt; but already should be faded, fatalistic and aged.

VIRGINIA WOOLF (1882-1941)

If I had my life to live over...
I'd dare to make more mistakes next time.
I'd relax. I would limber up.
I would be sillier than I have been this trip.

NADINE STAIR

Creativity is inventing, experimenting, growing,
taking risks, breaking rules, making mistakes,
and having fun.

MARY LOU COOK

... I am not a quitter. I will fight until I drop.... It is just a matter of having some faith in the fact that as long as you are able to draw breath in this universe you have a chance.

CICELY TYSON

Before you begin a thing remind yourself that difficulties and delays quite impossible to foresee are ahead. If you could see them clearly, naturally you could do a great deal to get rid of them but you can't. You can only see one thing clearly and that is your goal. Form a mental vision of that and cling to it through thick and thin.

KATHLEEN NORRIS, FROM "HANDS FULL OF LIVING"

Mahatma Gandhi

You may never know

Idealists... foolish enough to throw caution to the winds... have advanced mankind and have enriched the world.

EMMA GOLDMAN

You may never know what results come from your action. But if you do nothing, there will be no result.

MAHATMA GANDHI (1869-1948)

TRY AGAIN. FAIL AGAIN. FAIL BETTER.

SAMUEL BECKETT, FROM "WORSTWARD HO"

CHARACTER CONSISTS OF WHAT YOU DO
ON THE THIRD AND FOURTH TRIES.

JAMES A. MICHENER, FROM "CHESAPEAKE"

veryone
should have a chance
at a breathtaking piece
of folly at least once
in his life.

ELIZABETH TAYLOR, B.1932

You should nurse your dreams and protect
them through bad times and tough times to the
sunshine and light which always come.

WOODROW WILSON (1856-1924)

*Do not follow where the path may lead. Go, instead, where
there is no path and leave a trail.*

AUTHOR UNKNOWN

It is always the adventurers who accomplish great things.

MONTESQUIEU (1689-1755)

You must always be displeased by what you are. For where you were pleased with yourself there you have remained. Once you have said, "It is enough," you are lost. Keep adding, keep walking, keep advancing; do not stop, do not turn back, do not turn from the straight road.

ST. AUGUSTINE

N*ever fail yourself*
Never commit to limits...
Follow
the particulars of your spirit
as they pull you....

VERONICA D. CUNNINGHAM

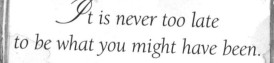

*It is never too late
to be what you might have been.*

GEORGE ELIOT (MARY ANN EVANS)
(1819-1880)

... if now is not the time to act, when will it be?

HILLEL (1ST CENTURY B.C.)

The distance is nothing; it is only the first step that is difficult.

MADAME DU DEFFAND

Perhaps this very instant is your time... your own, your peculiar, your promised and presaged moment, out of all moments forever.

LOUISE BOGAN (1897-1970)

G o confidently in the direction of your dreams!
Live the life you've imagined.

HENRY DAVID THOREAU (1817-1862)

You are everything that is, your thoughts, your life,
your dreams come true.
You are everything you choose to be. You are as
unlimited as the endless universe.

SHAD HELMSTETTER